Technology All Around Us

Aircraft

Kay and Andrew Woodward

A⁺

Smart Apple Media

First published in 2005 by Franklin Watts
96 Leonard Street, London EC2A 4XD

Franklin Watts Australia
Level 17/207 Kent Street, Sydney NSW 2000

Produced by Arcturus Publishing Ltd.
26/27 Bickels Yard, 151–153 Bermondsey Street, London SE1 3HA

Series concept: Alex Woolf, Editor: Alex Woolf, Designer: Simon
Borrough, Picture researcher: Glass Onion Pictures

Picture Credits:
Pictorial Press: 17.
Rex Features: cover and 15.
Science Photo Library: 4 (David Nunuk), 5 (US Library of Congress), 6
(Peter Menzel), 8 (Sally Bensusen), 10, 25 (NASA), 29 (NASA).
Topfoto: 13, 19, 20, 22.
TRH Pictures: 7, 9, 11, 12, 14, 16, 18, 21, 23, 24, 26, 27, 28.

Published in the United States by Smart Apple Media
2140 Howard Drive West, North Mankato, Minnesota 56003

Library of Congress Cataloging-in-Publication Data

Woodward, Kay.
Aircraft / by Kay and Andrew Woodward.
p. cm. — (Technology all around us)
Includes index.
ISBN 1-58340-724-3
1. Airplanes—Juvenile literature. I. Woodward, Andrew. II. Title. III. Series.

TL547.W7647 2005
629.133'34—dc22   2004065396

9 8 7 6 5 4 3 2 1

Contents

An aircraft is a flying machine. There are many different types of aircraft. Some are designed to carry hundreds of passengers on trips thousands of miles long. Others are designed to do tight aerial maneuvers or zoom across the sky in the blink of an eye.

Jets, helicopters, airships, seaplanes, and biplanes are just a few of the aircraft that fill the skies.

Aircraft can be divided into two main groups. Lighter-than-air aircraft, such as hot-air balloons, are filled with gases that are lighter than the air around them. These gases lift them up.

Heavier-than-air aircraft, such as airplanes, fly because of the shape of their wings and the way they travel through the air. They need a form of power, or thrust, to become airborne.

The First Flight

Before the 20th century, many people dreamed of taking to the skies, of swooping and gliding like birds. But no one had actually done it.

However, Orville and Wilbur Wright refused to keep their feet on the ground. On December 17, 1903, Orville made the first successful airplane flight. Although he stayed in the air for only 12 seconds and flew a distance of just 121 feet (37 m), the flight changed the world forever.

The Wright brothers' airplane, *Flyer I*, didn't have a pilot's seat, so Orville had to lie on the lower wing!

Looking Back

Fictional Flight

In 1873, one of writer Jules Verne's most famous books was published. *Around the World in Eighty Days* was the story of Phileas Fogg, who attempted to travel around the world in a balloon, a feat readers considered practically impossible.

Busy Skies

Since 1903, air travel has increased dramatically. At this very moment, thousands of aircraft are flying through the air.

Heathrow Airport in London, England, is the busiest airport in the world. Every day, about 640 airplanes take off from its runways. In 2004, more than 65 million passengers passed through its gates.

Airplanes like this Boeing 747 carry passengers around the world.

Looking Forward

Space Vacations

Every year, millions of people fly to far-off places on vacations. But soon they may be able to fly much farther than the Mediterranean, Hawaii, or New Zealand. Aircraft are being designed that will one day carry tourists into space.

Balloons and airships are large, graceful aircraft that move quietly through the skies. Large and hollow, they rise into the air when they are filled with hot air or gases—or both.

The main difference between the two types of aircraft is that an airship can be steered. Airships have engines and rudders, which help the pilot to take off and allow the aircraft to change direction. Balloonists have to go wherever the wind blows them.

Technology in Action

Record Breaker
It is March 21, 1999. The *Breitling Orbiter 3* is about to land in Egypt, completing its record-breaking, non-stop, around-the-world trip. The balloon works by using both hot air and helium. During the day, the sun warms the helium, which expands, causing the balloon to rise. During the cold night, the helium decreases in volume. Hot air is used to heat the helium so the balloon does not sink.

Hundreds of hot-air balloons take part in the annual Balloon Fiesta in Albuquerque, New Mexico.

Hot Air and Helium

Hot air is lighter than cold air because it is less dense. So, when balloons are filled with air that is hotter than the surrounding air, they rise.

A gas burner is used to heat the air inside the balloon. The more hot air there is inside the balloon, the higher it goes. When the balloonist stops firing the gas burner or opens a vent at the top of the balloon, it sinks.

The *Hindenburg* airship was filled with hydrogen—a highly flammable gas. While landing on May 6, 1937, the aircraft caught fire and exploded.

Looking Back

Fire Hazard!
Joseph and Etienne Montgolfier made the first successful hot-air balloon flight in 1783. But they didn't use a gas burner to make their balloon fly. They lit a fire underneath the balloon to heat the air inside!

Some balloons are filled with helium—a gas that is lighter than air—to make them rise. Helium-filled weather balloons rise high above Earth, where they monitor weather conditions and send information to scientists.

Steerable Aircraft

Unlike balloons, rigid airships contain a metal frame over which a strong material is stretched. Helium-filled bags inside the airship lift the aircraft. Engines propel the airship backward and forward. A rudder and elevators at the rear are used to steer the airship just like a submarine.

All airplanes require a number of features to fly. They need a power system to push them along the ground and through the air. They need wings to lift them and keep them airborne. They need a tail to steady them and flaps to steer them. Finally, they need wheels for taking off and landing.

Looking Back

Wright *Flyer*

The Wright brothers' biplane, *Flyer I,* weighed about 550 pounds (250 kg) and flew at roughly seven miles (11 km) an hour. Improvements in engines and design mean that although a modern Cirrus SR–22 G2 is four times as heavy, it can fly 16 times as fast as the biplane that first flew in 1903.

Some airplanes are modified so that they can land on water or snow. Seaplanes have floats instead of wheels, while airplanes that land on snow have skis.

Propellers provide enough power for small aircraft like this Beech Turbo Arrow IV.

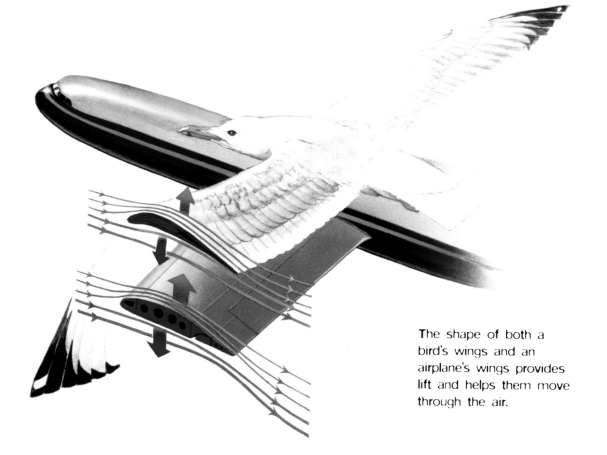

The shape of both a bird's wings and an airplane's wings provides lift and helps them move through the air.

Propellers

The first airplanes used propellers to fly. A propeller is a set of blades that spin around. In an airplane, a shaft connects the center of the propeller to the engine. When the engine is running, the shaft turns, causing the propeller to rotate.

The propeller's main job is to pull the aircraft along the runway fast enough for it to take off. It also pulls the airplane through the air and helps it to ascend.

How Wings Work

No matter how they are powered, all airplanes need wings to fly. These wings need a special shape: curved on top and flat on the bottom.

As the airplane moves, the curve of the wing means that air traveling over the top has to travel farther and faster than the air underneath. This creates lower air pressure above the wing and higher air pressure below the wing, which means that the wing lifts upward.

 Looking Forward

Future Fuel
Powered aircraft need fuel to fly. When Earth's supply of fossil fuels runs out, an alternative form of power will need to be developed.

The Boeing and Airbus companies currently are working on ways to use hydrogen, which is lighter than aircraft fuel. Scientists are developing fuel cells that produce electricity using hydrogen and oxygen.

The invention of the jet engine changed air travel forever. Jet engines are more powerful and more reliable than the piston engines that powered early propeller airplanes. They are also much easier to fix because they have fewer moving parts.

Jet engines have another huge advantage. Unlike piston engines, which do not work at extremely high altitudes because of the lack of oxygen, jet engines work very efficiently at great heights. They use less fuel at high altitudes, and because the air is thinner, they fly faster, too.

Outside view of a jet engine

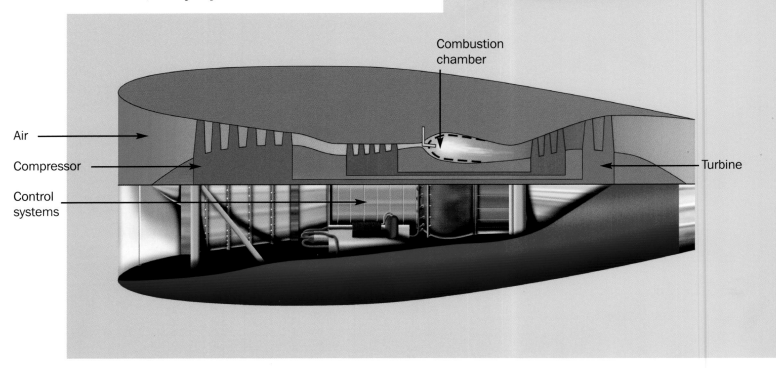

A diagram of a jet engine in action.

Air · Compressor · Control systems · Combustion chamber · Turbine

How a Jet Engine Works

Air is sucked into the front of a jet engine and is compacted, or compressed, by a spinning compressor. The compressed air is fed into chambers where fuel is added. The mixture of fuel and compressed air is then burned. When this burning jet of air and fuel flies out of the back of the engine, it pushes the engine—and the airplane—forward. The jet of air and fuel also passes through a turbine, turning it like a windmill and powering the compressor located at the front of the engine.

Looking Back

Invention of the Jet Engine

Frank Whittle, a British aeronautical engineer and pilot, invented the jet engine. At first, no one believed that his invention would work. The first jet engine was tested in 1937 and made its maiden flight in 1941. Whittle was honored with British knighthood in 1948.

Looking Forward

The Boeing 7E7 Dreamliner

The 7E7 is advertised as an efficient, eco-friendly, and people-friendly passenger jet. Designed to fly as fast as the fastest commercial airplanes, but using much less fuel, the first 7E7s are expected to carry passengers in 2008.

Jet engines that use a process called reheat create lots of thrust, producing a flame.

Less Noise Pollution

Jet engines are very noisy. For people who live near airports, this can be a major nuisance.

The high-bypass turbo fan was invented to cut down on noise pollution. A large fan is used to suck in much more air than a conventional jet engine, and much of this air is diverted around the jet engine. The extra air muffles the sound of the jet engine and burning gases that are propelled out the back. It also provides extra thrust.

Turboprops

Turboprops combine jet and propeller technology. A turboprop aircraft has a propeller, but instead of being powered by a piston engine, the propeller is powered by a jet engine.

A Bombardier Dash 8 Q400 has room for 70 passengers. Here, it flies high above the Grand Canyon.

Like early propeller planes, the propeller of a turboprop rotates, pulling the aircraft along the runway. But since a jet engine is more powerful than a piston engine, turboprops can be bigger than propeller planes.

How a Turboprop Works

A jet engine that is used to power a passenger jet or combat aircraft works by mixing air and fuel together. When this mixture is ignited, it shoots out of the back of the engine, pushing the airplane forward (see page 10).

A turboprop engine works in a similar way, but with one main difference. Instead of pushing the aircraft along, the power from the engine is used to spin the propeller, which pulls the aircraft along the runway and through the air.

Short-Haul Flights

Turboprops are ideal for short-haul flights—journeys of just a few hundred miles or less—that require small- or medium-sized passenger aircraft. Often, these are less frequently used routes between smaller cities and towns, or routes linking smaller regional airports to those in major cities.

Looking Back

The Invention of the Turboprop

Hungarian Gyorgy Jendrassik invented the turboprop engine in 1938. Although it was tested in 1940, production of Jendrassik's design was abandoned because of World War II.

Turboprops are small enough to fly into and out of small airfields, but they are powerful enough to carry a greater number of passengers than a small propeller plane. And because they fly faster, it takes less time to reach the destination.

The C-2A Greyhound can land in small spaces, such as on an aircraft carrier. A hook on the aircraft catches on a rope stretched across the flight deck to slow it down.

Alpine Airport

A small turboprop carrying a handful of eager skiers circles Courchevel Airport in the Alps—a notoriously difficult place to land. It is the steepest runway in the world and is only 1,263 feet (385 m) long. It can be reached only by helicopters or airplanes that are small enough to maneuver into tight spaces and powerful enough to take off again. The pilot circles, lines up with the runway, deploys the landing gear, and then descends.

WIGs

The wing-in-ground-effect vehicle, known as the WIG, is one of the most unusual vehicles ever invented. WIGs fly at very low altitudes, only a few feet above water, ground, snow, or ice.

Designed to carry large, heavy loads long distances over flat surfaces, WIGs usually land on and take off from water. Although they are usually regarded as low-flying aircraft, they can also be described as flying boats.

Looking Back

Ekranoplan

In the past, the majority of research and development into WIG aircraft was carried out in Russia. The Russian Ekranoplan—which means "sea skimmer"—was developed in 1961. Like other WIGs, the aircraft had very short wings. Ground effect was so strong that it needed only small wings to support it.

This picture shows the Ekranoplan WIG aircraft skimming above the surface of the sea.

The futuristic Pelican ULTRA is designed to take off from a runway but would need 76 wheels to support it while on the ground!

Looking Forward

Pelican ULTRA

The Pelican Ultra Large Transport Aircraft could be the biggest airplane ever built, with a wingspan of 492 feet (150 m). Designed to travel long distances over water, the Pelican would fly just 20 feet (6 m) above the waves but could climb to altitudes of more than 19,680 feet (6,000 m) over land. Best of all, it would be able to carry the same load as a container ship—at 10 times the speed.

Ground Effect

WIGs take advantage of the curious phenomenon of "ground effect," which was first discovered in the 1920s. If an aircraft flies very close to the water or ground, the surface beneath the wings stops the air from escaping, creating a cushion of air. This cushion is called ground effect. It is strong enough to keep the aircraft in the air.

Flying Low

It takes much less energy for an aircraft to fly in ground effect than it does to fly higher in the air. This means that WIGs are ideal for carrying large loads over long distances.

This early version of the Cierva C8 was built and flown in 1927.

An autogyro is a cross between a helicopter and an airplane. With a propeller for forward motion, an autogyro taxis for take-off like an airplane. Rotor blades lift the aircraft into the air.

Also known as a gyrocopter, this rotary-winged aircraft was the forerunner of the helicopter. Autogyros are still flown today because they are mechanically simpler than helicopters—making them cheaper to build and run.

Looking Forward

CarterCopter

The *CarterCopter* is a futuristic aircraft that aims to combine the efficiency of an airplane with the flexibility of a helicopter. It has a powered rotor for vertical takeoff and landing, and a set of small, fixed wings for high-speed cruising. Its designers predict that it will fly at speeds of more than 350 miles (560 km) per hour, at an altitude of 42,650 feet (13,000 m).

Unpowered Rotor

The rotor blades on an autogyro work much like the sails on a windmill, which turn when the wind blows them around. The autogyro's engine turns the propeller, which pulls the aircraft along the ground or through the air.

As the autogyro moves forward, air is forced through the rotor. This causes the rotor blades to turn and the autogyro to fly.

Because the autogyro's rotor blades are not powered, it does not take off and land vertically like a helicopter does. However, because the aircraft is so light, it can take off and land at low speeds and needs only a short runway.

Actor Sean Connery shown flying an autogyro in the James Bond film *You Only Live Twice*.

Lookouts

Early autogyros were flown like kites from the backs of ships or submarines. The motion of the ship pulled them through the air, making the rotor blades turn and eliminating the need for engines.

These autogyros served the same purpose as old-fashioned crow's-nests in sailing ships. A lookout sitting in the autogyro had a good view of the surrounding sea and could give early warning of approaching enemy vessels.

Looking Back

<< **Aerial Filming**

Spanish aeronautical engineer Juan de la Cierva invented the autogyro in 1923. One of his aircraft—the Cierva C–30A—could fly at speeds of less than 9.4 miles (15 km) per hour. It was used to monitor traffic during major sporting events.

A helicopter is an aircraft that is capable of very precise movements. Using rotor blades, it can take off and land vertically, fly in virtually any direction, or hover without moving. Most airplanes cannot perform any of these operations.

Helicopters can land almost anywhere—on mountaintops, on the roofs of buildings, and even on ships. As long as there is an empty space slightly bigger than the helicopter itself, it can land. Helicopters are often used as air ambulances, transporting people who are very ill or critically injured to a hospital as quickly as possible.

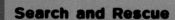

Technology in Action

Search and Rescue
In April 2004, the Belfast coast guard is called to search for two canoeists missing in rough seas. Within minutes, a helicopter crew is assembled and the aircraft lifts off. The two men are soon located and lifted to safety.

The Boeing C-47D Chinook is powerful enough to lift a 2.75-ton (2.5 t) truck!

How Helicopters Fly

A helicopter's engine drives its rotor. As the rotor spins, it lifts the aircraft into the air. Each of the rotor blades is hinged, allowing it to move up and down as it spins.

This MV-22 Osprey tiltrotor is being directed to a landing area on the USS *Essex* aircraft carrier.

Tilting the helicopter's rotor provides thrust, making it fly in a certain direction. For example, if the rotor is tilted forward, the helicopter will fly forward.

However, the rotor creates a problem. When it spins quickly in one direction, it forces the body of the helicopter to spin in the other direction.

This problem is solved by adding a small rotor to the tail of the aircraft. This smaller rotor prevents the helicopter from spinning around like a top. It also helps to steer.

Twin-Rotor Helicopters

The first helicopters were big enough to carry only one or two people. But improvements in engine design have led to the development of bigger helicopters that have two large rotors to support their weight. The rotors spin in opposite directions, which is called contra-rotating.

 Looking Forward

The Tiltrotor
The Bell Agusta 609 tiltrotor is a revolutionary aircraft that looks like an airplane with a rotor mounted on each wing. The BA609 combines the vertical takeoff and landing capabilities of a helicopter with the speed of a turboprop airplane.

19

Defense departments around the world fund the design of many aircraft that are developed for use in military situations. Some of these pioneering designs influence the design of civilian aircraft.

Military aircraft can be divided into three main categories: combat, transport, and reconnaissance.

The F-16 Fighting Falcon can refuel in mid-air, enabling it to fly long distances without landing.

Combat Aircraft

During a war, combat aircraft play a vital role in attacking and defending territory. They must be able to fly at high speed to enter and depart from enemy airspace as quickly as possible. They must be able to fly at low altitudes to avoid detection by radar. And they must be able to perform complicated maneuvers quickly and safely.

The first Eurofighter Typhoons were delivered in 2003. These aircraft have a maximum speed of Mach 2 (twice the speed of sound) and carry an array of weapons.

Transport Aircraft

Military action often takes place in distant countries. This means that thousands of troops and vast quantities of equipment, food, vehicles, and other supplies have to be carried long distances.

Transport aircraft are large and powerful, capable of lifting heavy loads. The Lockheed C-130 Hercules can carry more than 22 tons (20 t)—about the same weight as 12 cars.

Looking Back

The Battle of Britain

Military aircraft were first used effectively during World War II. The Battle of Britain, which took place in the skies above Britain in 1940, was a turning point in the war. The Spitfire and the Hurricane were two of the famous propeller aircraft that took part in aerial combat.

Looking Forward

UCAVs

In the future, it is possible that all combat aircraft will be pilotless. UCAVs (unmanned combat aerial vehicles) such as the Boeing X–45A will be operated remotely, without risking pilots' lives.

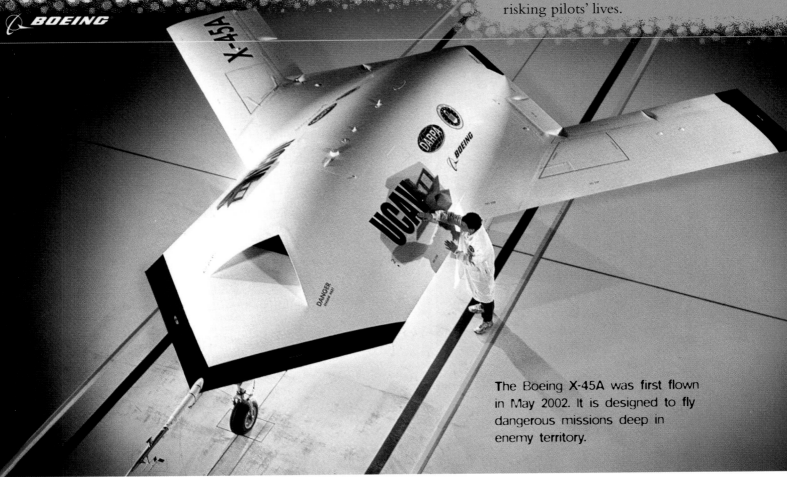

The Boeing X-45A was first flown in May 2002. It is designed to fly dangerous missions deep in enemy territory.

Reconnaissance Aircraft

In the past, aircraft were often used to fly over enemy territory and make observations. They flew high and fast in order to escape detection. However, reconnaissance missions are now usually carried out by satellites or unmanned aircraft such as the RQ-IA Predator, which was used during military action in Bosnia, Kosovo, and Iraq in the 1990s and early 21st century.

VTOL Aircraft

Vertical takeoff and landing (VTOL) aircraft are a familiar sight during war. Although some are designed to land on a runway, they can all take off and land vertically.

VTOL aircraft can land in places that are inaccessible to an airplane. They can be flown deep into enemy territory and remain hidden, ready to move into action at a moment's notice. They are also ideal for landing on and taking off from an aircraft carrier.

Although it flies in a different way, the Harrier can hover and make small movements like a helicopter. This AV-8B Harrier is hovering above an aircraft carrier.

Technology in Action

Emergency Landing

It is June 7, 1983. A British Royal Navy Harrier pilot flies across the sea, struggling at the controls of his Harrier Jump Jet. It is an emergency situation—the airplane has suffered a major electronics failure. The pilot's only options are to land or to eject. Suddenly, he spots a container ship that is moving slowly across the water. Minutes later, and with only minor damage to the aircraft, the pilot and his airplane have landed safely on the Spanish freighter *Alraigo.* The Spanish crew can hardly believe their eyes.

How VTOL Aircraft Fly

VTOL aircraft do not use the same technology as helicopters. Instead, they use jet engines and are equipped with thrust-vectoring nozzles. These direct the power from the jet engine to enable slow, precise movements.

When pointed downward, the nozzles provide the thrust necessary for takeoff. This downward thrust also allows the aircraft to land vertically or to hover. If the nozzles are pointed forward, the aircraft flies backward. When the nozzles are pointed backward, the aircraft is propelled forward at high speed. As with all other airplanes, wings provide lift when the aircraft moves forward.

Looking Back

The Flying Bedstead
During the development of technology for VTOL flight, British engineers worked with a metal frame instead of an actual aircraft. It was nicknamed the "Flying Bedstead" and made its first untethered flight in August 1954.

Even though the Flying Bedstead looked nothing like an airplane, it flew!

The One and Only

The Harrier Jump Jet was developed in the 1950s. Despite many other attempts to develop new VTOL aircraft, at the beginning of the 21st century, the Harrier Jump Jet is still the only VTOL aircraft in active service and manufactured in great numbers.

A supersonic aircraft flies faster than the speed of sound. At sea level, the speed at which sound travels through the air is 760 miles (1,225 km) an hour. This speed varies according to air temperature. The speed of sound is also known as Mach 1.

Most aircraft are subsonic—that is, they fly slower than the speed of sound. Because of the costs involved in building and operating them, only a few airplanes have been designed that can achieve supersonic speeds.

The Sound Barrier

Scientists once thought that there was a physical barrier to supersonic flight. It seemed that as an aircraft neared the speed of sound, it became harder to fly. It was as if it needed a huge amount of power to accelerate from subsonic to supersonic speeds. This process was known as "breaking the sound barrier."

We now know that there is no physical sound barrier, and although aircraft need more thrust to fly faster, they do not need a huge surge of energy to exceed the speed of sound.

Looking Back

Going Supersonic

On October 14, 1947, the *Bell X1* rocket plane, flown by U.S. test pilot Chuck Yeager, was the first aircraft to achieve supersonic speeds. It had a revolutionary flying tail, which stabilized the aircraft at extremely high speeds.

On January 21, 1976, the first commercial Concorde flights took place, with flights from London to Bahrain, and Paris to Rio de Janeiro.

If it is built, the hypersonic *X-43B*, or *Hyper-X*, could be a reusable launch vehicle for spacecraft.

Concorde

To date, the Concorde is the only successful supersonic passenger plane to be built. Shaped like a dart, with large wings and a moveable nose cone, it could travel through the air at up to Mach 2 (twice the speed of sound).

The nose cone was raised for supersonic flight and pointed downward to allow the pilots to see the runway for takeoff and landing.

Flying high above Earth's surface, the Concorde could travel from London to New York in just three and a half hours. It went out of service in 2003 because it was too expensive to run. There was no new technology to replace it.

Looking Forward

Hypersonic Aircraft

When aircraft achieve speeds greater than Mach 5, they are said to be traveling at hypersonic speed. The U.S. Air Force has already developed hypersonic aircraft. How much faster can they go? Only time will tell.

Not all aircraft are designed to travel at record-breaking speeds or zoom hundreds of passengers from continent to continent. Many small aircraft are designed with just one thing in mind—fun!

These aircraft can be divided into two main groups: powered and unpowered. Light aircraft and microlights are powered by engines. Gliders and hang gliders soar on the wind and are pulled back to Earth by gravity.

The pilots of these light aircraft are performing aerobatics for audiences on the ground. Here, they loop-the-loop.

Light Aircraft

Small propeller aircraft are known as light aircraft. They usually carry between one and four people and are ideal for learning to fly. Many people choose to fly light aircraft because they are cheaper to buy or rent and cheaper to run than larger, faster aircraft.

Microlights

Microlights are the lightest form of powered aircraft. Some have fixed wings like airplanes, while others have canopies like hang gliders.

Usually made out of fiberglass and fabric, the wings can be easily folded away and stored instead of taking up space in a hangar.

Looking Forward

Microlight Broadband

British engineers are eager to develop microlight technology that can be used to provide broadband Internet connections in sparsely populated areas or for people on the move.

Solar-powered microlights would hover 12 miles (20 km) above the earth, receiving and sending computer signals. Each would be far cheaper than a satellite performing the same job.

Gliders

As their name suggests, gliders do not fly—they glide. First, an airplane tows them along the runway and into the air. When released, they gradually glide back down to earth, riding currents of warm air, called thermals, just like a bird!

Hang gliders are fabric canopies, usually with room for just one person to hang beneath. They are flown from high ground, again gliding on warm air currents.

Technology in Action

Sandstorm!

It is 2000, and award-winning microlight pilot Colin Bodill is attempting to fly solo around the world. Suddenly, he hears a dreadful noise and realizes that his exhaust pipe has cracked.

This could be disastrous. He is flying over the Saudi Arabian desert, where sandstorms are raging. For two hours, Colin holds his broken aircraft together, battling against the sand and the wind. At last, he lands safely. His microlight might be extra light, but it is also strong.

There is enough room in this hang glider for two people to enjoy the view.

The *Gossamer Albatross* was an aircraft that flew by pedal power.

Aircraft technology is constantly changing as engineers and designers look for ways to make aircraft faster, higher-flying, easier to pilot, cheaper to run, more environmentally friendly, and safer.

And it is not just large companies that research and develop aircraft. Often, aircraft are built by enthusiasts who dream of breaking records or just want to make their own amazing flying machine.

Looking Back

Unidentified Flying Objects (UFOs)

Since World War II, there have been countless sightings of UFOs over the Nevada Desert in the U.S. It is rumored that brand-new, top-secret aircraft are tested in this area, and it is likely that the strange objects in the sky came from Earth—not space.

This morphing-wing plane is designed to fly like the peregrine falcon. NASA scientists hope that the aircraft will be swooping and soaring like a bird by 2030.

Test Pilots

From enormous, double-decker passenger jets to helicopters built from a kit, every aircraft must be flown and tested before it is allowed to fly. It is a test pilot's job to make sure that it is safe.

Pushing the Boundaries

Can you imagine an airplane that is pedaled like a bicycle? Or an aircraft that flies for weeks fueled only by sunlight? Did you know that both of these aircraft have already flown?

Looking Forward

The Ansari X Prize

Future aircraft may fly not just in the air above Earth, but in outer space, too. The Ansari X prize represented a great leap toward this goal. This was a competition that asked applicants to design and build a vehicle capable of carrying three adults to a height of 60 miles (100 km), returning to Earth and then taking three more passengers into space within two weeks. The prize was won in October 2004 by an aircraft called *SpaceShipOne*. With aircraft design, the sky is no longer the limit. . . .

In 1979, professional cyclist Bryan Allen pedaled his way across the English Channel in a super-light aircraft called the *Gossamer Albatross*. The aircraft's enormous, lightweight wings helped to keep it in the air at low speeds.

Meanwhile, the National Aeronautics and Space Administration (NASA) is funding research into the solar-powered *Pathfinder*, which is remotely controlled from the ground. Powered by the sun's light, it can fly at high altitudes for weeks on end, recording data for scientific projects.

1483 Leonardo da Vinci designs a helicopter.

1783 Joseph and Etienne Montgolfier make the first hot-air balloon flights.

1852 A steam engine is used to power the first airship.

1860s Ponton d'Amecourt flies steam-powered helicopters.

1903 Orville and Wilbur Wright make the first powered, manned flights.

1907 The first helicopter is flown by French inventor Paul Cornu.

1909 Louis Blériot becomes the first person to fly across the English Channel.

1919 John Alcock and Arthur Whitten Brown make the first transatlantic flight.

1937 The jet engine is invented.

1938 The turboprop engine is invented.

1939 Igor Sikorsky flies the first practical helicopter.

1939–45 The development of fighter and bomber planes during World War II changes the nature of warfare.

1947 Chuck Yeager flies faster than the speed of sound.

1954 The Boeing 707 first flies. It is the earliest successful commercial airliner.

1966 The Harrier Jump Jet first flies.

1969 Concorde—the first supersonic passenger jet—takes flight.

1979 A pedal-powered plane is flown across the English Channel.

1986 Dick Rutan and Jeana Yeager fly nonstop around the world on one tank of fuel in an aircraft called *Voyager*.

1999 The *Breitling Orbiter 3* becomes the first balloon to travel nonstop around the world.

2003 Concorde goes out of service.

2004 *SpaceShipOne* wins the $10 million Ansari X Prize.

aerial combat Fighting between aircraft that takes place in the air.

aeronautical engineer A person who designs and builds aircraft and their systems.

air pressure The force exerted by air molecules. The greater the number of molecules (or the higher the temperature), the higher the air pressure.

altitude The measurement of height above the ground.

biplane An aircraft with two sets of wings.

civilian aircraft An aircraft used by the public instead of military personnel.

commercial aircraft Aircraft such as airliners that are owned and operated for the purpose of making money.

compressor The part of a jet engine that condenses air before it is combusted with fuel to provide thrust. The compressor is turned by a turbine.

deploy To move something into place in order to use it.

eco-friendly Something that does not damage the environment.

elevators Small wings mounted on the tail of an airplane that are used to keep the aircraft level in flight.

flaps A part of a wing that can be extended to allow an airplane to fly slowly when landing and taking off.

fossil fuel Mineral-based oil products, such as gas, kerosene, or diesel oil, that are used as fuel.

gas burner The part of an engine that allows the controlled burning of fuel within a stream of compressed air.

helium A very light gas.

hydrogen An extremely light but flammable gas.

jet engine An engine that compresses air, mixes it with fuel, and then burns it to produce a thrust strong enough to push an aircraft.

landing gear The part of an aircraft that carries the wheels used during storage, landing, and takeoff.

Mach 1 The speed of sound.

maiden flight The first flight of a particular type of aircraft.

piston engine A small, cheap, lightweight engine often used to power light aircraft.

propeller A wing-shaped blade attached to an engine that is used to pull an aircraft through the air.

radar An electronic system that uses radio waves to detect the position of aircraft.

reconnaissance Airborne observation of an area for military purposes.

rotor blades The horizontal rotating wings that enable a helicopter to fly.

rudder The vertical tail fin of an aircraft that is used to help steer.

shaft The part of a drive system used for transferring the energy of an engine to a propeller or rotor.

solar power The sun's energy used as a fuel.

tail The rear part of an aircraft, which carries the rudder and elevators.

taxi Move forward before takeoff or after landing.

thrust The force that moves an aircraft through the air.

thrust-vectoring nozzles Parts of a VTOL aircraft that allow the jet's thrust to be directed either horizontally or vertically, enabling it to fly or to hover.

turbine A fan-like machine rotated by the hot exhaust gases of a jet engine, which is used to turn the compressor.

vent A flap in a balloon that can be opened to release gas into the atmosphere.

volume The amount of space taken up by something.

Further Information

Further Reading
Butterfield, Moira. *Supreme Machines: Aircraft*. London: Franklin Watts, 2003.

Gibbs, Lynne, and Neil Morris. *Mega Book of Aircraft*. North Mankato, Minn.: Chrysalis, 2003.

Nahum, Andrew. *Flying Machine*. New York: Dorling Kindersley, 2004.

Polin, C. J., and Caryn Jenner. *First Flight*. New York: Dorling Kindersley, 2003.

Web sites
http://www.howstuffworks.com
A site that provides information on airplanes, helicopters, and hang gliders.

http://www.flight100.org/history_intro.html
A Web site run by the American Institute of Aeronautics and Astronautics that celebrates the history of aviation.

http://www.concordesst.com/history/historyindex.html
A Web site dedicated to the supersonic passenger plane Concorde.

Index

Page numbers in **bold** refer to illustrations.